T0008888

HOCKEY

SCORE WITH STEM!

By Craig Ellenport

Consultant: Tammy Englund, science educator

BEARPORT
PUBLISHING

Minneapolis, Minnesota

Credits

Cover and Title Page, © Dan Kosmayer/Shutterstock; background image, © Vera Larina/Shutterstock; 4, © GreenLand Studio/Shutterstock; 5, © Adam Cairns/TNS/Newscom; 6, © Mitrofanov Alexander/Shutterstock; 7 top, © Alexandr Grant/Shutterstock; 7 bottom, © Shoreline Publishing Group; 8, © Robert Nyholm/Shutterstock; 9 top, © Sergii Kumer/Dreamstime; 9 bottom, © Frank Jansky/Icon Sportswire/Newscom; 10, Shooter Bob Square Lenses/Shutterstock; 10–11, © Lucky Business/Shutterstock; 12, © Luckey Business/Shutterstock; 13 top, © Cornelia Naylor/BurnabyNow.com; 13 bottom, © Jon Sorenson/Novacaps.com; 14, © Richard Ulreich/Cal Sports Media/AP Images; 15 top, © John Locher/AP Images; 15 bottom, © Petr Sznapka/CTK/AP Images; 16, © AP Photo; 16–17, © John Modesti/Dreamstime; 18–19, © Todd Berkey/The Tribune-Democrat/AP Images; 19, © Linda Williams/Dreamstime; 20, © Andreas Gora/picture-alliance/AP Images; 21 (2), © Andreas Gora/picture-alliance/AP Images; 22, © Shooter Bob Square Lenses/Shutterstock; 23, © Shu Ba/Shutterstock; 24, © Brent Clark/CSM via Zuma Wire/AP Images; 25, © Jason Szenes/UPI/Newscom; 26, © Julio Cortez/AP Images; 27, © Bill Kostroun/AP Images; 31, © Brent Clark/CSM via Zuma Wire/AP Images

Bearport Publishing Company
Minneapolis, Minnesota
President: Jen Jenson
Director of Product Development: Spencer Brinker
Senior Editor: Allison Juda
Associate Editor: Charly Haley
Designer: Colin O'Dea

Produced by Shoreline Publishing Group LLC
Santa Barbara, California
Designer: Patty Kelley
Editorial Director: James Buckley Jr.

Library of Congress Cataloging-in-Publication Data

Names: Ellenport, Craig, author.
  Title: Hockey : score with STEM! / By Craig Ellenport.
  Description: Minneapolis, Minnesota : Bearport Publishing Company, [2022] |
  Series: Sports STEM | Includes bibliographical references and index.
Identifiers: LCCN 2021003695 (print) | LCCN 2021003696 (ebook) | ISBN
  9781636911786 (library binding) | ISBN 9781636911854 (paperback) | ISBN
  9781636911922 (ebook)
Subjects: LCSH: Hockey--Juvenile literature. | Science--Study and
  teaching--Juvenile literature. | Technology--Study and
  teaching--Juvenile literature.
Classification: LCC GV847.25 .E45 2022 (print) | LCC GV847.25 (ebook) |
  DDC 796.356--dc23
LC record available at https://lccn.loc.gov/2021003695
LC ebook record available at https://lccn.loc.gov/2021003696

For more information, write to Bearport Publishing, 5357 Penn Avenue South, Minneapolis, MN 55419. Printed in the United States of America.

Contents

Hockey and STEM

The fans in the hockey arena jump to their feet as the forward streaks toward the goal. His skates cut into the ice, and he pushes the puck along with his curved stick. As he nears the goal, he pulls the stick back and then whips it forward. *Wham!* The puck smashes into the goalie's pads. What a **save**! The fans scream and cheer!

But do the fans know the whole story? With players zooming along the ice, hockey is a fast sport—and STEM is a part of all the action!

SCIENCE: Thanks to physics, players can make the puck glide across the ice or fly through the air at amazing speeds.

TECHNOLOGY: Video recordings and wearable tech have changed what players, coaches, and fans can learn.

ENGINEERING: Amazing arenas and smooth ice rinks are designed with engineering.

MATH: Information about teams and players is gathered as numbers called **stats**. A winning score is just the beginning!

Goalie Sergei Bobrovsky makes a save!

Hockey's Famous Puck

The referee waits at center ice for a **face-off**. When the two players are in position, he holds out a flat, round disk—the puck. As the referee blows his whistle, he drops the puck onto the ice. The players' sticks crash together! They push the puck back and forth until . . . *zing!* One player slides the puck across the ice to a teammate. The action is on!

Today's pucks are 3 inches (7.6 cm) across and weigh about 6 ounces (170 gm).

Cold and Flat

For more than 140 years, ice hockey players have used flat, rubber pucks. The flat sides help pucks glide easily across the ice. But hockey also has a chilly secret to help pucks move—they are frozen when they enter play! A frozen puck doesn't bounce as much, giving players more control. As the rubber warms up, it gets energy from the heat. The more energy in a puck, the more it bounces.

National Hockey League (NHL) pucks have a logo printed in ink that changes color when frozen. As the puck warms up, the logo changes from purple to black. This means it's time to change pucks!

RONDELLE DE MATCH OFFICIELLE

Gary B Bettman
COMMISSIONER

OFFICIAL GAME PUCK

© NHL

Slap Shot Science

The forward takes a perfect pass from her teammate and skates toward the goal. A defender rushes between the forward and the goalie. The forward comes to a sudden stop. Eyeing her target, she lifts her stick high in the air behind her. Her powerful arms swing the stick back down, unleashing a high-speed slap shot. She scores!

Defenders stand in the way of a forward heading toward the goal.

High Speed!

When a player raises their stick and swings it back down, it has **kinetic energy,** or the energy of motion. This energy transfers to the puck and causes it to **accelerate**. The faster the stick is moving when it hits, the faster the puck will go. Slap shots move so fast that goalies sometimes have trouble seeing them!

The fastest slap shot ever recorded came in a 2020 American Hockey League game. Martin Frk of the Ontario Reign hit a shot that reached 109.2 miles per hour (175.7 kph)!

Speed on Ice

The forward digs his skates into the ice and rushes toward the goal. The defender does the same as he chases after the forward. Ice chips fly as the players pick up speed. Just as the forward starts to shoot, the defender catches up and blocks the shot! He was fast enough to get there in time.

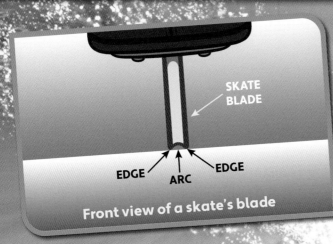

SKATE BLADE

EDGE   ARC   EDGE

Front view of a skate's blade

The Secret in the Blades

Skaters can thank physics for their speed on slippery ice. Hockey skates have blades with sharp edges on either side of a small **arc**. As the skate moves across the ice, **friction** between the edges of the blade and the surface of the ice creates heat. This heat melts a tiny amount of the ice. So, the skate is actually moving on a very thin layer of water, making for a smooth ride!

To stop while skating, a player also needs to use friction. The skater does this by changing the position of their feet, pushing the edge of the skates hard into the ice. This **pressure** creates the friction needed to stop.

Wearable Tech

The first game for the team's new center seems to be going well, but her coach wants to be sure. The coach checks a tablet from the bench. During the next break, the coach calls the center over and says, "You're doing great. Keep up the hard work!" How does the coach know that?

The more a coach knows, the more they can do to help the team.

Getting Helpful Info

Sensors attached to players' gear can wirelessly gather and send all kinds of **data** to tablets and computers at the bench. The technology allows coaches to see where players go on the ice and how fast they're skating. They can also watch a player's heart rate, breathing, and body temperature. All this data can help prevent injuries and make sure athletes are playing at their best.

Sensors can be placed on players' helmets, pads, or skates.

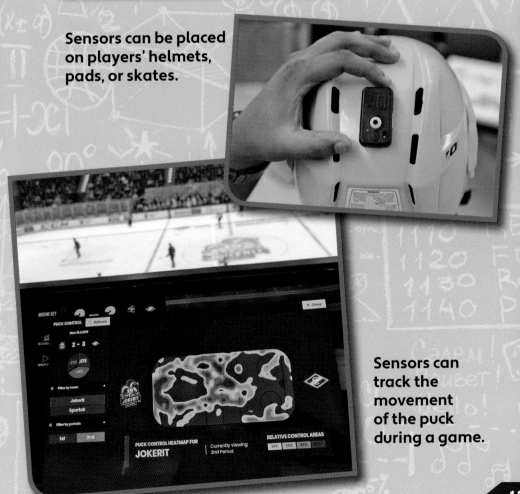

Sensors can track the movement of the puck during a game.

Smile for the Camera

The forward skates back to the bench. He just played a long shift on the ice but wasn't able to get in position to take a good shot. He knows he'll have another chance later, so he checks a video screen. The player is not watching a TV show— he's watching himself in action! The video can help him play better. How does it work?

NHL players can watch video from the games they are playing in.

Review to Improve

Pro hockey teams have coaches who record all the action on the ice. Then, they edit the footage and share specific plays with members of the team. The videos can be played over and over, as many times as needed. By reviewing their performances on video, players can decide what they should do differently in the future.

Some tech can let you watch virtual hockey anywhere.

Coaches, players, and fans aren't the only ones who use video replay. During a game, referees can also check video to see whether a player scored a goal or if a penalty was called correctly.

Guardian of the Goal

The goalie stares out through the bars of his mask as a forward gets ready to shoot. The goalie quickly checks to make sure his heavy leather gloves are open and his thick leg pads are facing the shooter. As the puck flies toward him, the goalie blocks the shot. He didn't feel a thing, except the satisfaction that he had stopped the puck!

Protection from the Puck

For many years, hockey goalies did not wear much protection. Leg pads were made of leather stuffed with cotton, and masks were not popular with goalies until the 1960s. But thanks to technology, goalies today are safer than ever. Modern gear is made of strong, lightweight materials. Fiberglass helmets and metal masks cover goalies' heads. Leg pads are thin but very strong, thanks to new plastics. Goalies even wear chest protectors made from Kevlar—the same material used to make bulletproof vests!

To be safe, pro
goalies make sure
their helmets and
pads fit perfectly.

Ice Cleanup

The horn sounds, ending the second period. All the players leave the ice to take a break. But their skates have carved up the surface of the ice, leaving scrapes, ridges, and bumps. The ice must be smooth for the players in the next period. It's time for the Zamboni!

Zamboni in Action

A Zamboni looks like a **mechanical** monster, slowly gliding over every inch of the rink. A blade inside the machine shaves and removes the top layer of ice. At the same time, a vacuum sucks up any dirt and water on the ice. Then, the Zamboni releases a thin layer of hot water that quickly freezes to create a smooth, icy surface. Game on!

In the 1940s, Frank Zamboni owned a skating rink. Back then, making the rink's surface clean and flat for skaters took many hours. To solve this problem, he invented a machine that quickly smoothed the surface of the ice. It worked so well that Zambonis are still used in ice rinks around the world.

Quick Change!

A basketball game has just ended, and fans are making their way out of the arena. Tomorrow, two teams will play hockey on an ice rink in the same arena. How can a sports stadium go from hoops to hockey? By using smart engineering!

From Wood to Ice

The hockey rink in many sports arenas is actually found *under* the basketball court! When a basketball game ends, a crew of more than 60 workers removes the wood court and its layer of padding. This reveals a sheet of ice, kept frozen by a grid of cold pipes underneath the smooth surface. The crew adds a few more layers of ice on top and then paints on the lines and circles needed for the hockey game. Then, even more ice goes on top of that, and the hockey rink is ready!

1 Crews first remove the wooden panels that formed the basketball court.

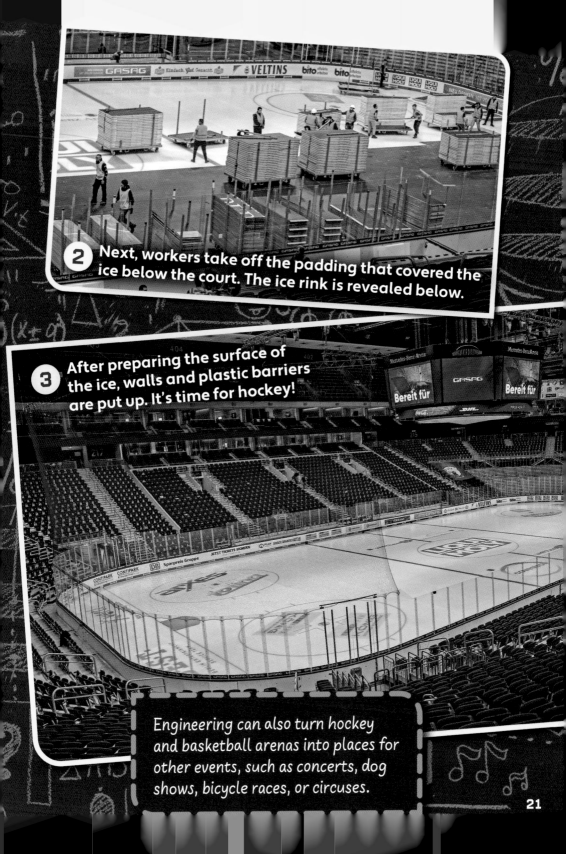

2 Next, workers take off the padding that covered the ice below the court. The ice rink is revealed below.

3 After preparing the surface of the ice, walls and plastic barriers are put up. It's time for hockey!

Engineering can also turn hockey and basketball arenas into places for other events, such as concerts, dog shows, bicycle races, or circuses.

A Rink of Shapes

As the centers for each team get ready for the face-off, they meet in the middle of a circle. Their defenders line up on the blue lines behind them. Farther back, the goalies stand near the goal lines. There are shapes and lines everywhere. A hockey rink is packed with geometry!

The opening of an NHL goal cage is a rectangle 6 feet (1.8 m) wide and 4 ft (1.2 m) high.

Circles and Lines

An NHL hockey rink is in the shape of a rectangle with rounded corners. Thick blue lines in each half of the rink show where each team's defensive zone begins. Red lines mark center ice and the goal lines near each end. Red circles are used for face-offs. In front of each goal is an arc called a goalie crease. All these shapes on the ice have their own special purpose!

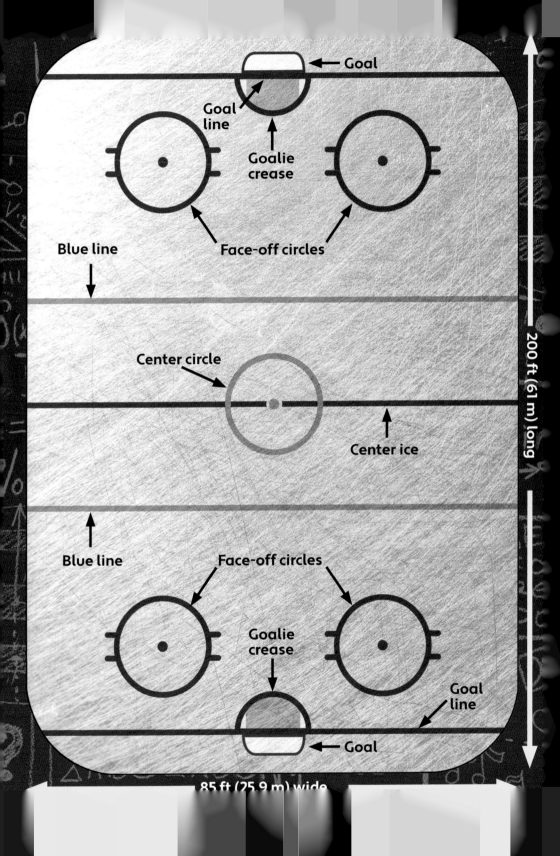

Teaming Up for Points

The center skates ahead, guiding the puck and avoiding defenders. She sees a wing farther up the ice and slides the puck to her teammate. The winger receives the pass and looks up at the goal. *Snap!* Her shot whizzes over the goalie's shoulder and smacks into the back of the net! The winger has scored the goal, but both she and the center get a point.

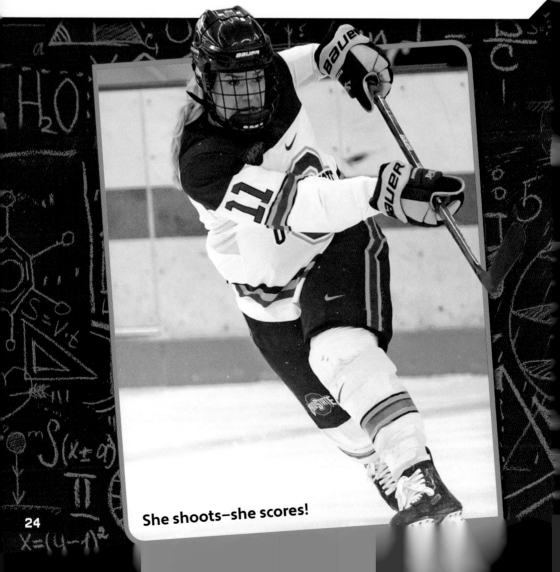

She shoots—she scores!

Points Champion

Hockey teams win games by scoring the most goals. But hockey players earn points for goals and assists. An assist is when a player makes a pass or takes a shot that helps a teammate score a goal. To calculate a player's total points for a game, a season, or a career, add their goals and assists. Wayne Gretzky is known as the Great One because he holds the all-time NHL record for most points. In his career, Gretzky scored 894 goals and had 1,963 assists. His career points add up to 2,857.

Wayne Gretzky

NHL Career Points Leaders
Wayne Gretzky	2,857
Jaromir Jagr	1,921
Mark Messier	1,887

How Low Can You Go?

As the final horn sounds, the goalie leaps happily into the air. She has only let in two goals. Her teammates have scored five goals, so their team has won the game 5–2! The goalie's teammates gather around her and congratulate her on her saves. And the coach tells the goalie that she may have improved her stats! What stats might those be?

Figuring Out GAA

The stat called goals against average (GAA) is the average number of goals scored against a goalie per 60 minutes of playing time, which is the standard length of a game. Having a low GAA means a goalie has been successful at stopping shots. To calculate GAA, multiply the number of goals let in by 60, then divide that number by the number of minutes played. NHL goalies hope to have GAAs of 3.0 or less.

Tuukka Rask

In 2020, Tuukka Rask had the best career GAA of all active NHL goalies. He had allowed an average of only 2.26 goals per game.

Do the Math!

It's time to do some hockey math! Learn how to calculate four types of stats below. Then, do the math to find out which players had the best stats.

Adding Points

Add each player's goals and assists to see who has the most total points.

1. Which player had the most points?

PLAYER	GOALS	ASSISTS
Connor McDavid	41	75
Patrick Kane	48	63
Alex Ovechkin	60	52

Save Percentages

To find the percentage of saves a player made, divide the number of saves a goalie made by the number of shots they faced. This stat is shown in a decimal.

2. Which goalie had the best save percentage?

PLAYER	SAVES	SHOTS FACED
Ben Bishop	1,236	1,323
Jordan Binnington	748	807
Carey Price	1,791	1,952

Per-Game Averages

A per-game average is a number that shows how well a player did in more than one game. To find it, divide the player's total points by the number of games played.

3. Which player had the highest points-per-game average?

PLAYER	POINTS	GAMES
Steven Stamkos	99	79
Nikita Kucherov	85	65
Patrick Kane	79	62

Plus-Minus Score

The plus-minus score shows which players are helping their team the most. When an **even-strength goal** is scored, the players on the ice for the scoring team get a plus, and those on the ice for the other team get a minus.

4. Subtract the minuses from the pluses to find out which of these players had the higher plus-minus score.

PLAYER	PLUSES	MINUSES
Bobby Orr	176	47
Bobby Hull	164	51

Answers:
1. McDavid's total of 116 points was higher than Kane's 111 and Ovechkin's 112.
2. Bishop's percentage of .934 was the highest. Binnington came in at .927, ahead of Price's .918.
3. It was close, but Kucherov's 1.31 points per game average was above Kane (1.27) and Stamkos (1.25).
4. With a plus-minus of 129, NHL Hall of Famer Bobby Orr's score was above the plus-minus of fellow superstar Bobby Hull's 113.

Glossary

accelerate to change speed; in physics, acceleration is a measurement of the rate at which an object changes speed or direction

arc a part of the outside of a circle

data information often in the form of numbers

even-strength goal a goal scored when each team has the same number of skaters on the ice

face-off a part of the hockey game used to restart play; two players battle for a puck dropped by a referee

friction the rubbing of one thing against another

kinetic energy energy that is in motion

mechanical having to do with machines

pressure physical force

save when the goalie stops a goal from being scored

sensors electronic devices that gather and record information

stats short for statistics; information stated as numbers

Read More

Dufresne, Emilie. *The Science of Ice Hockey (Play Smart).* New York: KidHaven Publishing, 2021.

Martin, Brett S. *STEM in Hockey (STEM in Sports).* Minneapolis: Abdo Publishing, 2018.

Williams, Heather. *Hockey: A Guide for Players and Fans (Sports Zone).* North Mankato, MN: Capstone Press, 2020.

Learn More Online

1. Go to **www.factsurfer.com**

2. Enter "**STEM Hockey**" into the search box.

3. Click on the cover of this book to see a list of websites.

Index

About the Author

Craig Ellenport has written many books about sports, and he is a co-author of *NHL: The Official Illustrated History*. Ellenport never played professional hockey, but he was a member of his junior high school math team!